Name: ____

HABITS OF A SUCCESSFUL MIDDLE SCHOOL MUSICIAN

TUBA

A Comprehensive Method Book for Years Two, Three, and Beyond

SCOTT RUSH

JEFF SCOTT • EMILY WILKINSON

RICH MOON • KEVIN BOYLE

EDITED BY MARGUERITE WILDER

Available Editions:

Flute	G-9142
Oboe	G-9143
Bassoon	G-9144
Clarinet	G-9145
Bass Clarinet	G-9146
Alto Saxophone	G-9147
Tenor Saxophone	G-9148
Baritone Saxophone	G-9149
Trumpet	G-9150
French Horn	G-9151
Trombone	G-9152
Euphonium	G-9153
Baritone TC	G-9154
Tuba	G-9155
Mallets	G-9156
Percussion	G-9157
Conductor's edition	G-9158

GIA PUBLICATIONS, INC.
CHICAGO

Habits of a Successful Middle School Musician – Tuba Edition
Scott Rush • Jeff Scott • Emily Wilkinson • Rich Moon • Kevin Boyle

G-9155
ISBN: 978-1-62277-192-9

7404 S. Mason Avenue, Chicago, IL 60638
www.giamusic.com

Contents

Welcome to the *Habits of a Successful Musician* series. This supplemental method book was written to help you establish an effective daily routine that will ultimately lead to great music making. As you perfect the various components of playing, it is important that they only serve as a means to an end, for being the chance to call your performances *artistic*.

This method book is primarily a warm-up, chorale, rhythm and sight-reading curriculum. Each exercise has a very specific purpose. Once these skills have been mastered, the technique of playing must logically progress to more musical concepts. Let's begin our musical journey!

The book is divided into thirteen sections:

- Stretching and Breathing
- Interval Studies
- Whole Tone Scale Studies
- Attack Pattern
- Scale and Arpeggio Studies
- Lip Slurs
- Articulation Exercises
- Dynamic Exercises
- Chord Progressions
- Chorales
- Rhythm Vocabulary
- Sight-Reading Exercises by Level
- Audition Sight-Reading by Time Signature

Tips for Individual Practice

- Prior to the warm-up, listen to two minutes of a recording of your favorite artist on your instrument; then try to imitate the artist's sound.
- Set goals for each practice session and devise a logical order of things to cover, beginning with a well-planned warm-up.
- Strive to cover as many Components of Playing as possible, starting with the Four Ts: Timing, Tuning, Tone, and Technique.
- Begin your practice session with stretching, followed by breathing exercises. Brass players should also buzz on the mouthpiece.
- Your initial warm-up material should come from the first eight sections of the book.
- Practice in twenty-minute increments, with five minutes of rest between.
- *Stay relaxed*—tension is your worst enemy.
- Remember that a few minutes of quality practice is better than any minute of bad, unfocused practice. As the saying goes: *Only perfect practice makes perfect*.
- As part of rehearsing for auditions, use the Audition Sight-Reading section to improve your reading skills.
- When sight-reading, establish a slow, logical tempo that will enable you to play everything on the page while maintaining a steady tempo/pulse.
- Record yourself and critique your work. Gain a personal knowledge of your strengths and weaknesses.
- Finish your practice session by playing something fun (maybe your favorite piece). Brass players should warm down by playing long tones down to the lowest note on their instrument.

I. Warm-Up

1. Stretching and Breathing

2. Interval Studies

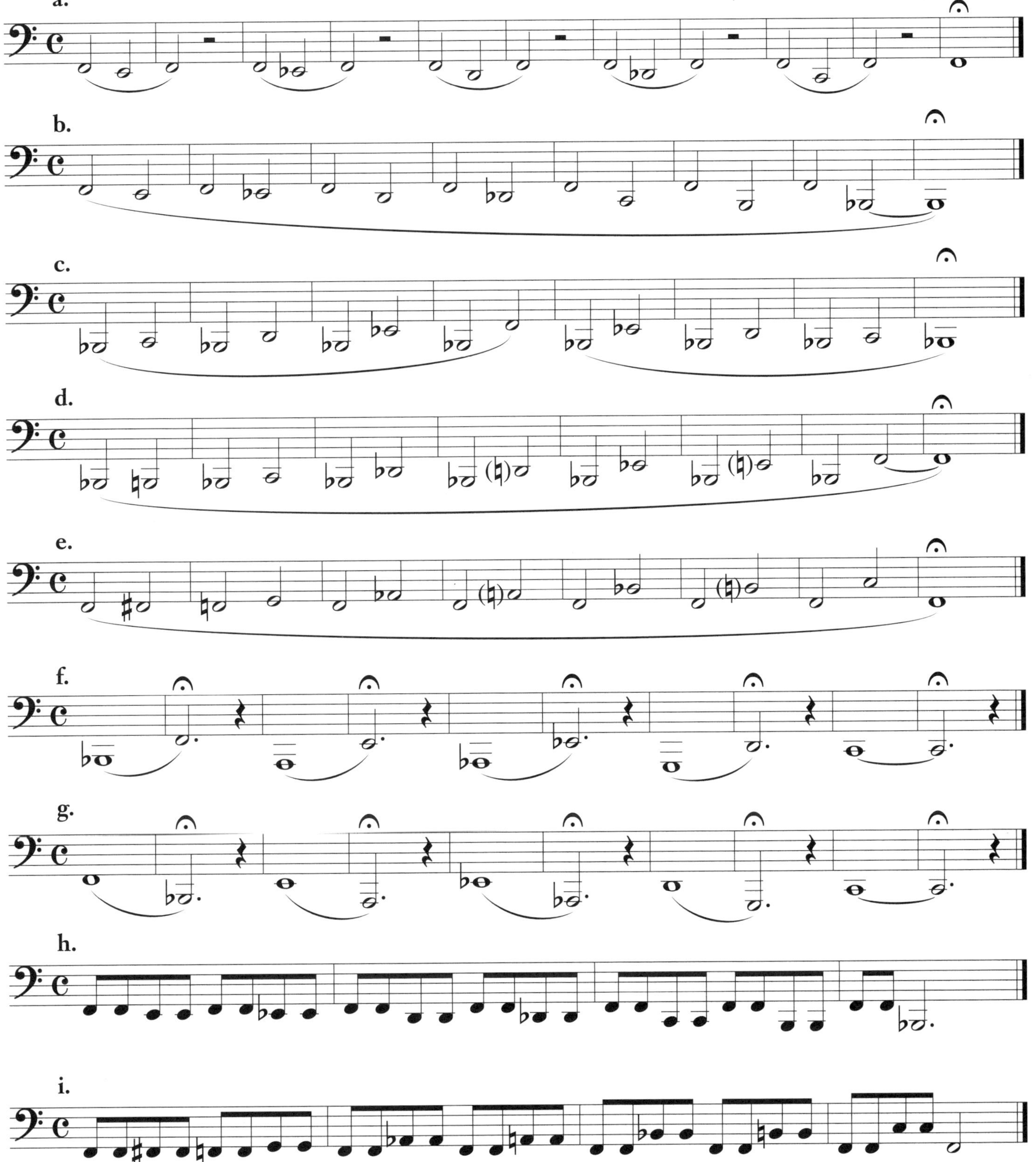

3. Whole Tone Scale

4. Attack Pattern

a. Balance, Blend, Tuning, Tone

5. Scale and Arpeggio Studies

a. B♭ Scale

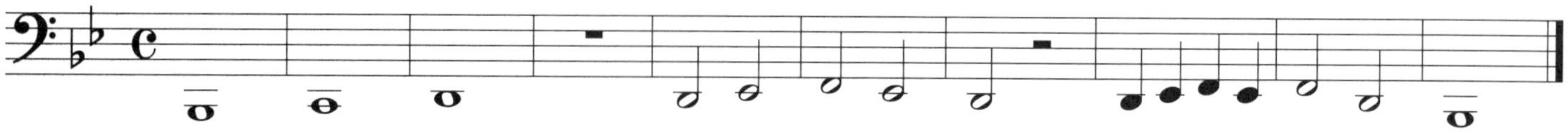

b.

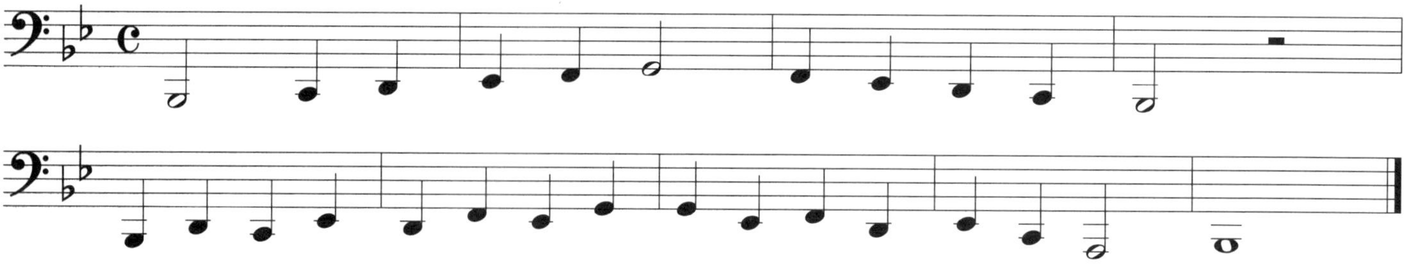

c.

d. B♭ Scale

Major Scale

Arpeggio

Thirds

Chromatic Scale

a. E♭ Scale

b.

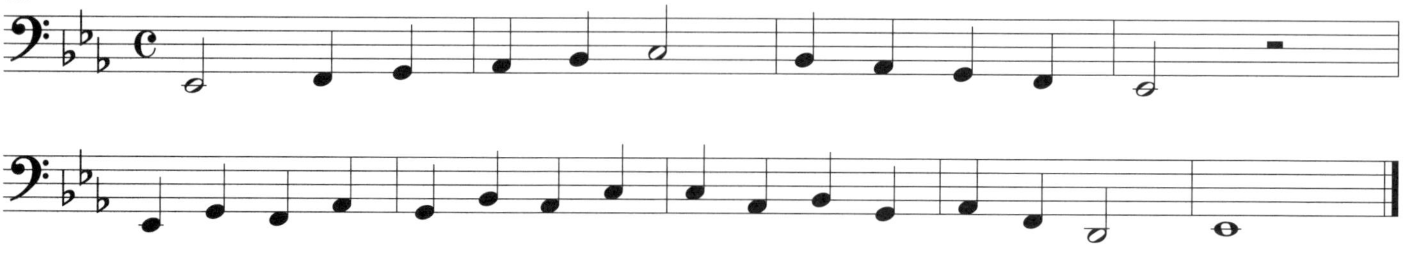

c.
d. E♭ Scale
Major Scale
Arpeggio
Thirds
Chromatic Scale
a. A♭ Scale
b.
c.

d. A♭ Scale
Major Scale
Arpeggio
Thirds
Chromatic Scale
a. D♭ Scale
b.
c.
d. D♭ Scale
Major Scale
Arpeggio
Thirds
Chromatic Scale

a. G Scale

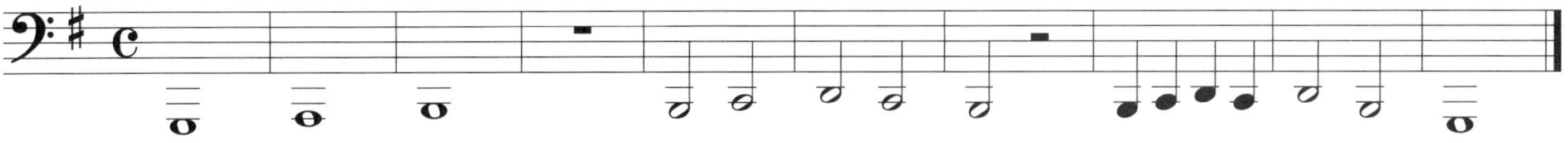

b.

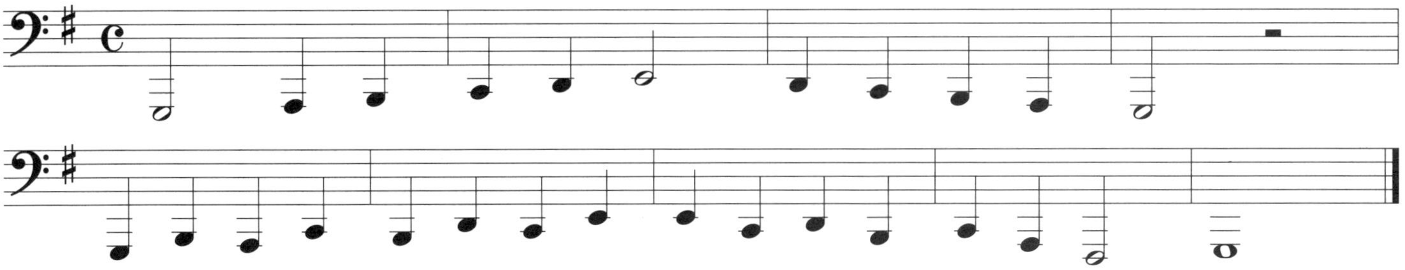

c.

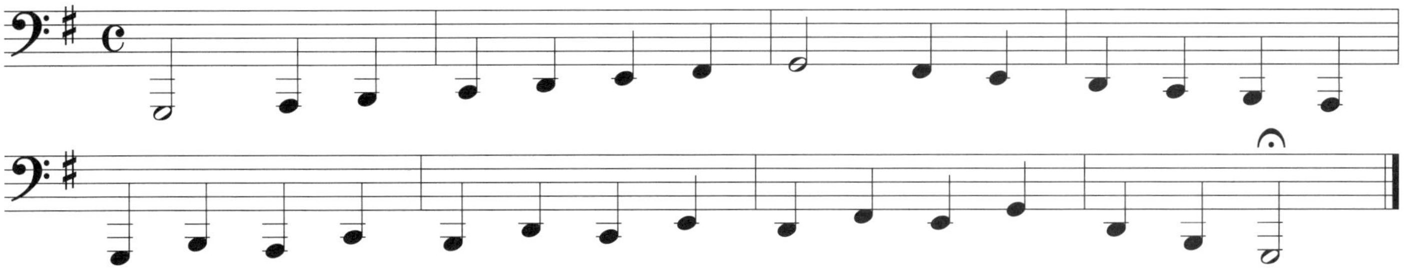

d. G Scale

Major Scale

Arpeggio

Thirds

Chromatic Scale

a. C Scale

b.

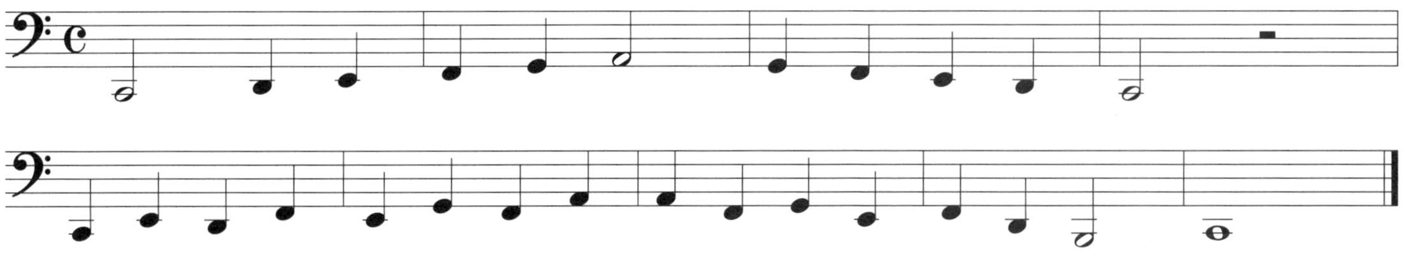

c.
d. C Scale
Major Scale
Arpeggio
Thirds
Chromatic Scale
a. F Scale
b.
c.

d. F Scale

6. Lip Slur Exercises

a.

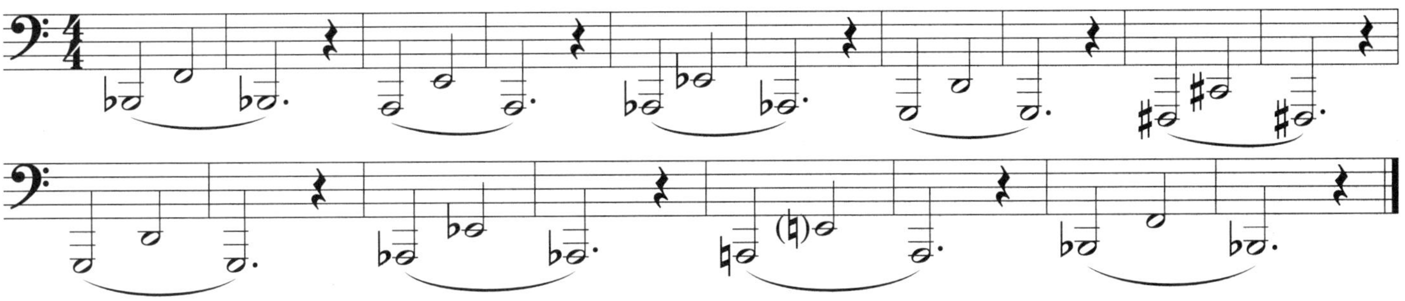

(‡)

b.

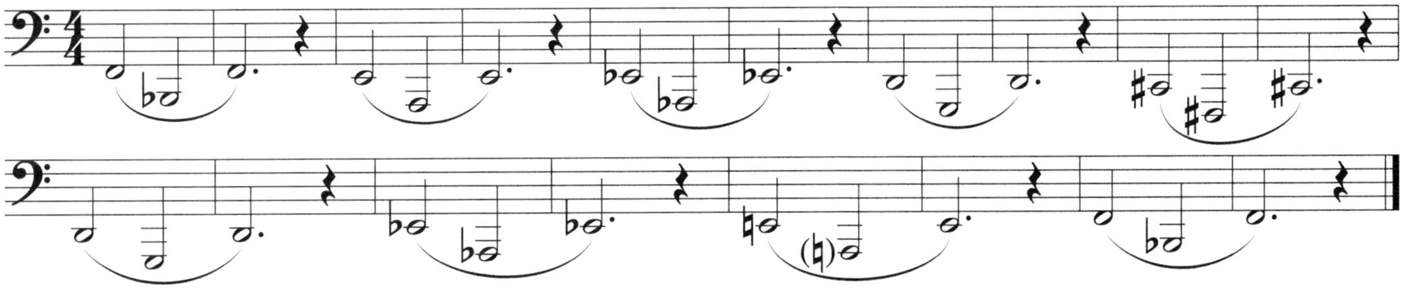

(‡)

c.

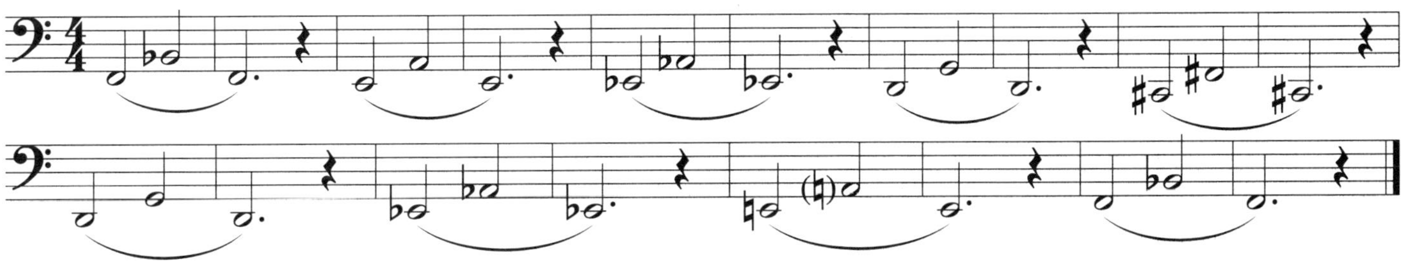

(‡)

d.
e.
f.
g.

h.

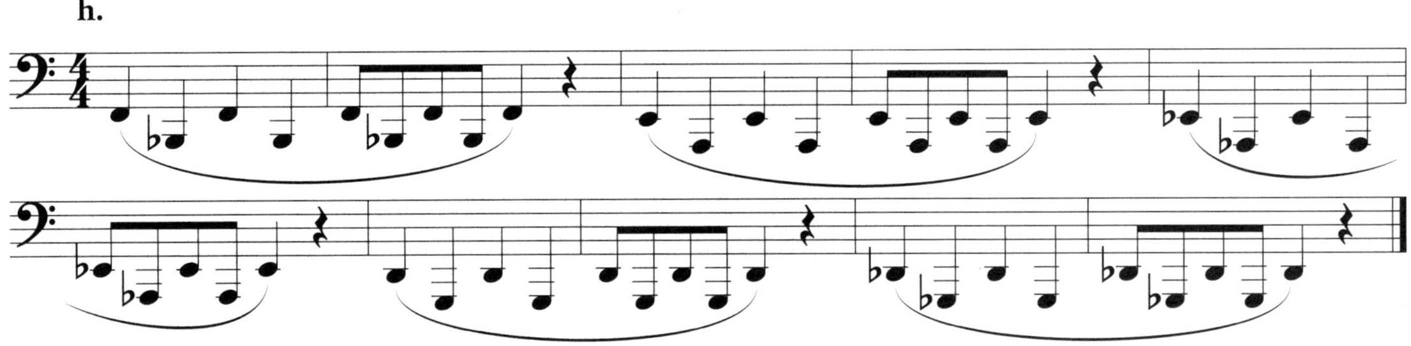

i.

7. Articulation Exercises

a.

b.

c.

d.

e.
f.
g.
h.
i.
j.
k.

l.

8. Dynamics

a.

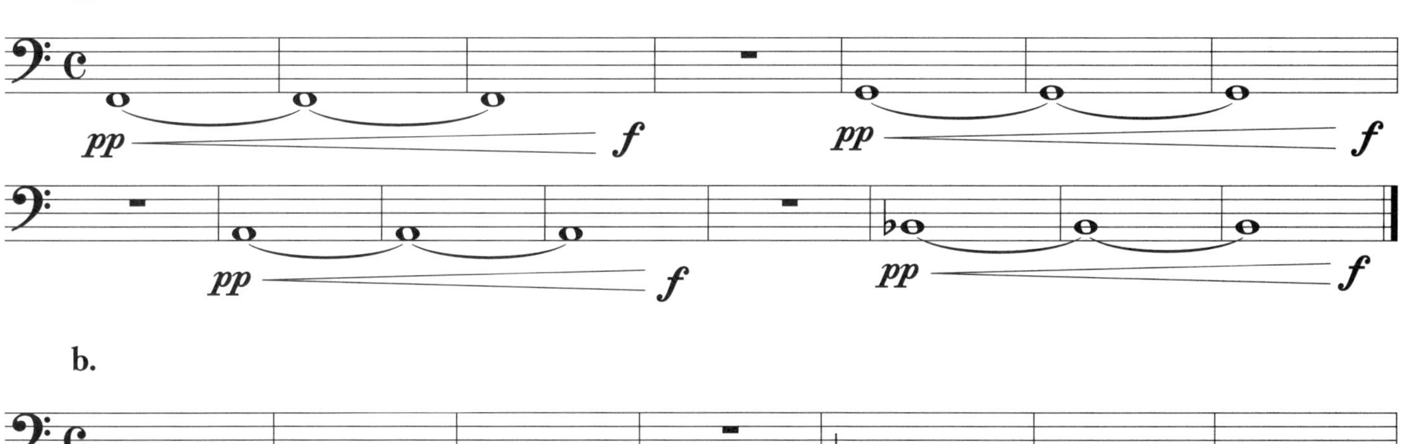

b.

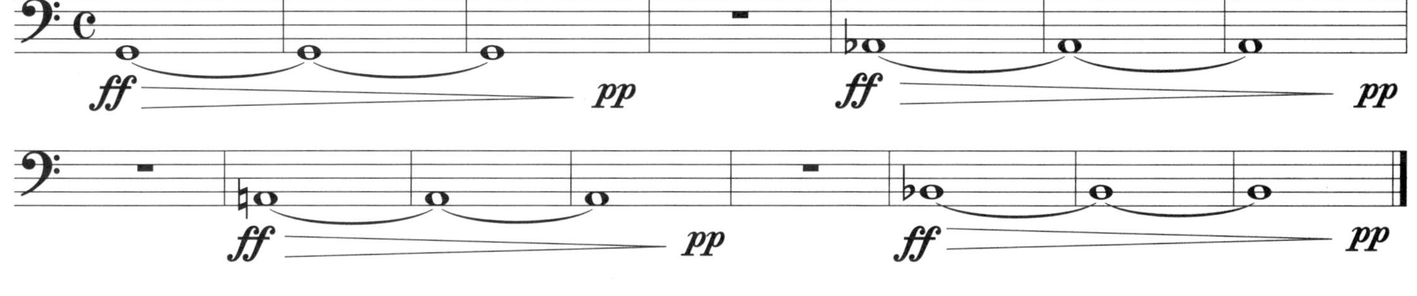

c.

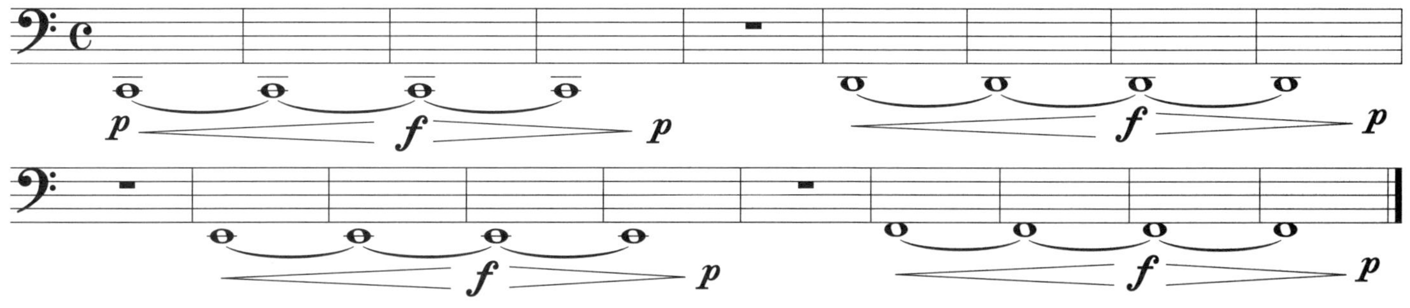

d.

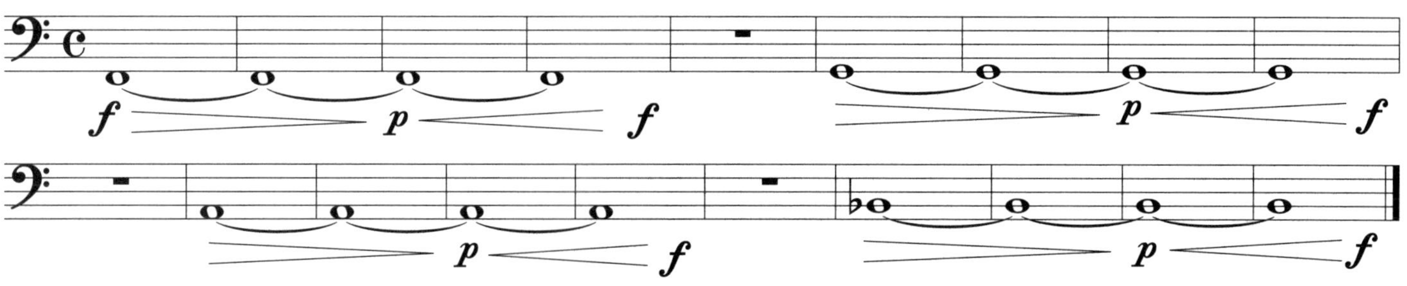

f *p* *f* *p* *f*

p *f* *p* *f*

e.

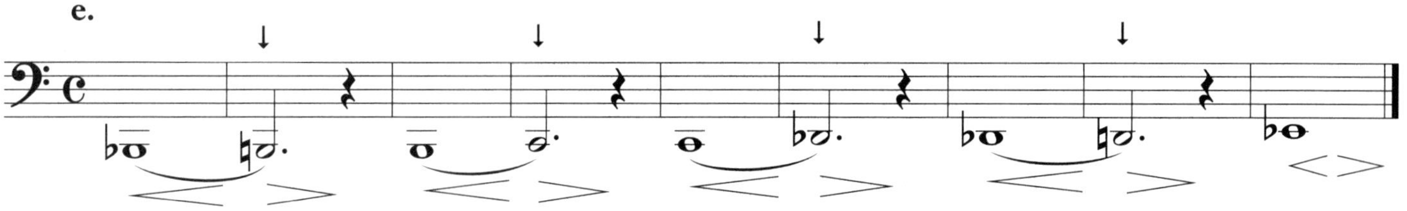

f.

fp *fp* *fp* *fp* *fp*

g.

pp *ff* *pp* *ff* *pp* *ff* *pp* *ff*

h.

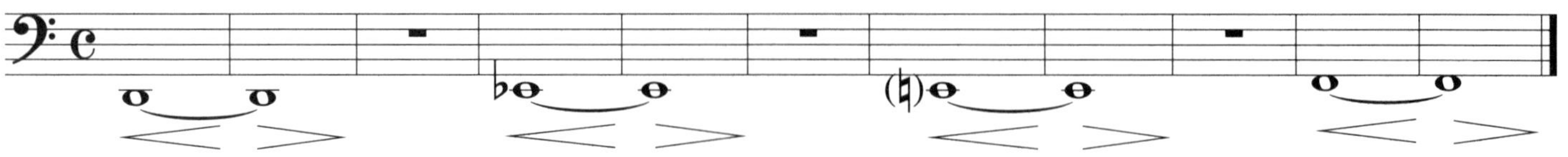

(♮)

i.

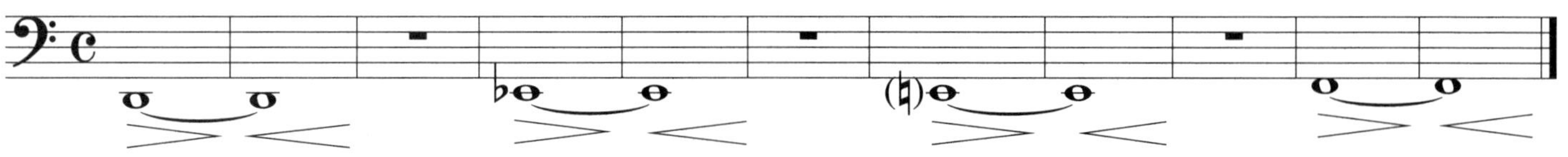

(♮)

9. Chord Progression

a.

b.

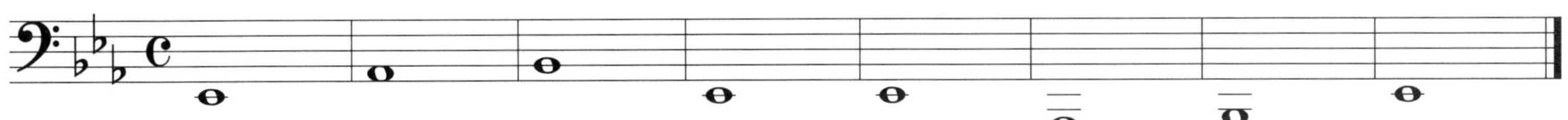

c.

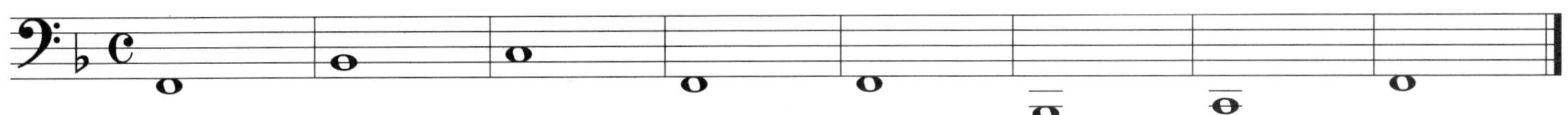

d.

e.

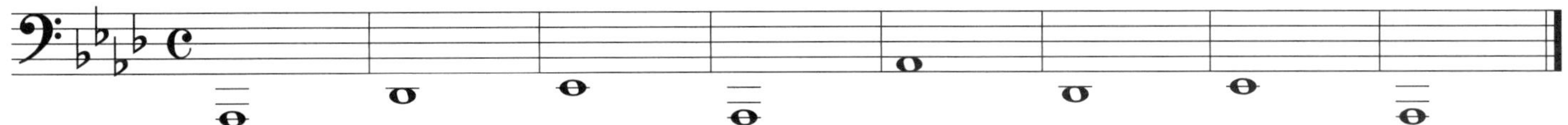

f.

g.

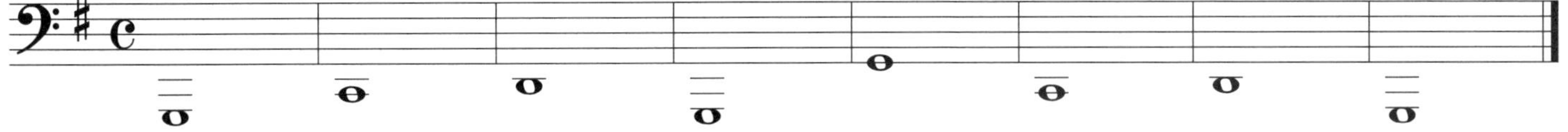

II. Chorales

Chorale #1

Chorale #2

Chorale #3

Chorale #4

Chorale #5

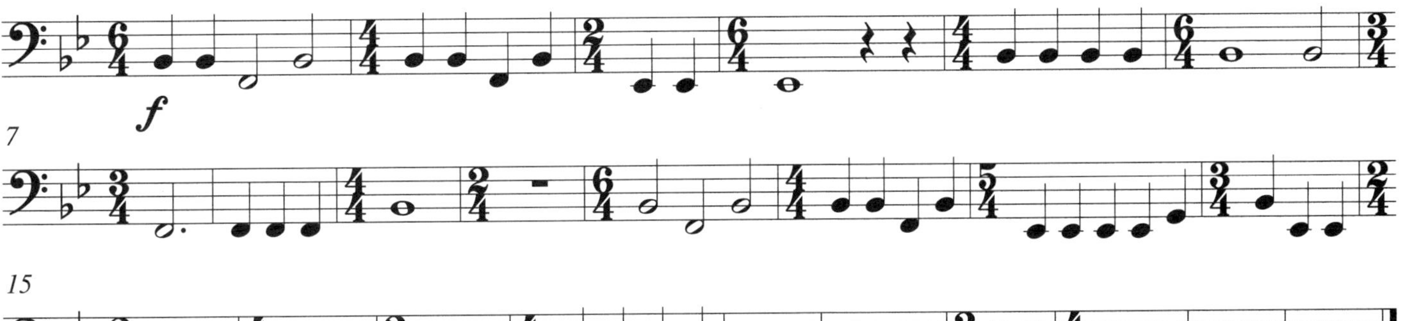

Chorale #6

Chorale #7

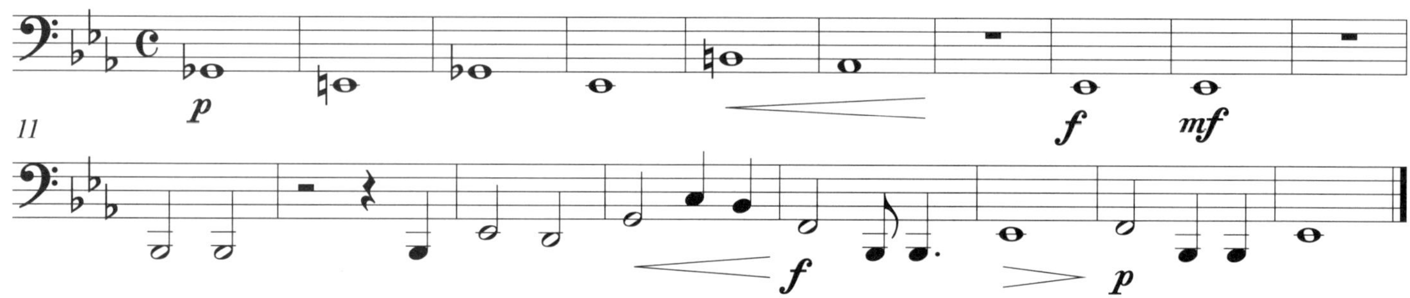

Chorale #8

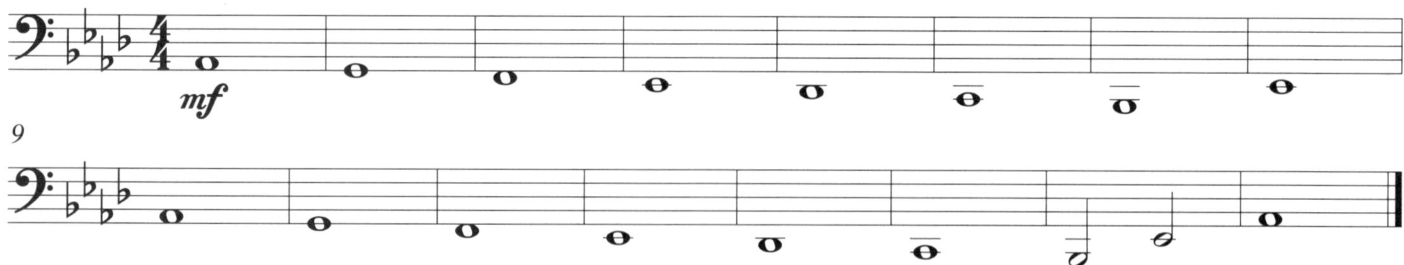

Chorale #9

Chorale #10

Chorale #11

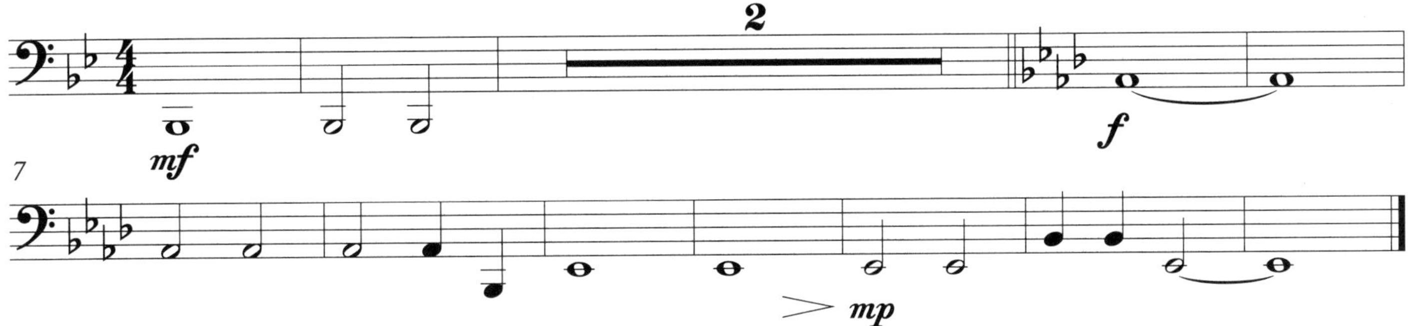

Chorale #12

Chorale #13

Chorale #14

Chorale #15

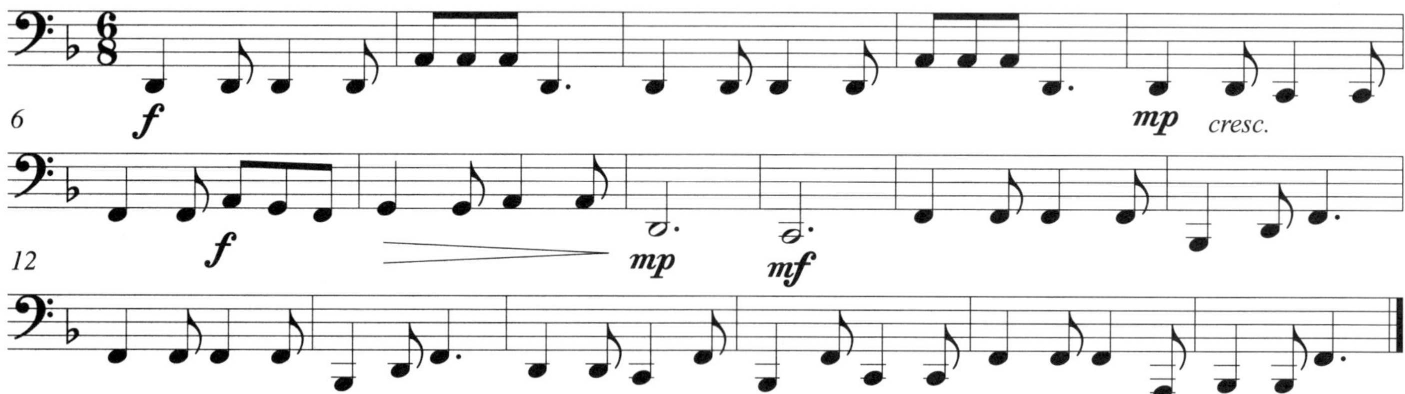

III. Rhythm Vocabulary

6a.
6b.
7a.
7b.
8a.
8b.
9a.
9b.

10a.
10b.
11a.
11b.
11c.

12a.

12b.

13a.

13b.

14a.

14b.

15a.
15b.
16a.
16b.
17a.
17b.

18a.
18b.
19a.
19b.
20a.
20b.
21a.
21b.

22a.
22b.
23a.
23b.
24a.
24b.
25a.
25b.

26a.
26b.
27a.
27b.
28a.
rit.
28b.
rit.

29a.
29b.
30a.
30b.
31a.
31b.
32a.
32b.
33a.
33b.

34a.
34b.
35a.
35b.
36a.
36b.
37a.
rit.
37b.
rit.
38a.
38b.

39a.
39b.
40a.
40b.
41a.
41b.
42a.
42b.
43a.
43b.

44a.
44b.
45a.
45b.
46a.
46b.
47a.
47b.

48a.
3
48b.
49a.
49b.
50a.
50b.
51a.
51b.

52a.
52b.
53a.
53b.
54a.
54b.
55a.
55b.

56a.
56b.
57a.
57b.
58a.
58b.

IV. Sight-Reading by Level

You will notice that section four has very few annotated dynamics or articulations. This was done to allow the concepts of *timing* and *pulse* to be the primary focus while sight-reading in this section. Other "components of playing" will be added in section five.

9.
10.
11.
12.
13.
14.
15.
16.

17.
18.
19.
20.
21.
22.
23.
24.
25.

26.
27.
28.
29.
30.
31.
32.
33.

34.
35.
36.
37.
38.
39.
40.

41.
42.
43.
44.
45.
46.

47.
48.
49.
50.
51.
52.
53.
54.

55.

56.

57.

58.

59.

60.

61.

62.

63.

64.

65.

66.

67.

68.

69.

70.
71.
72.
73.
74.
75.
76.
77.
78.

79.
80.
81.
82.
83.
84.
85.

86.
87.
88.
89.
90.
91.
92.

93.

94.

95.

96.

97.

98.

99.

100.

101.

V. Audition Sight-Reading by Time Signature

9.
f
mp
f rit.
10.
f
mp
f
rit.
11.
mf
p
f
12.
mf
f
rit.
p
13.
3
mp
f
p
14.
3
mp
f
mp
rit.
15.
mp
f
mp
16.
3
mp
f
mp
f

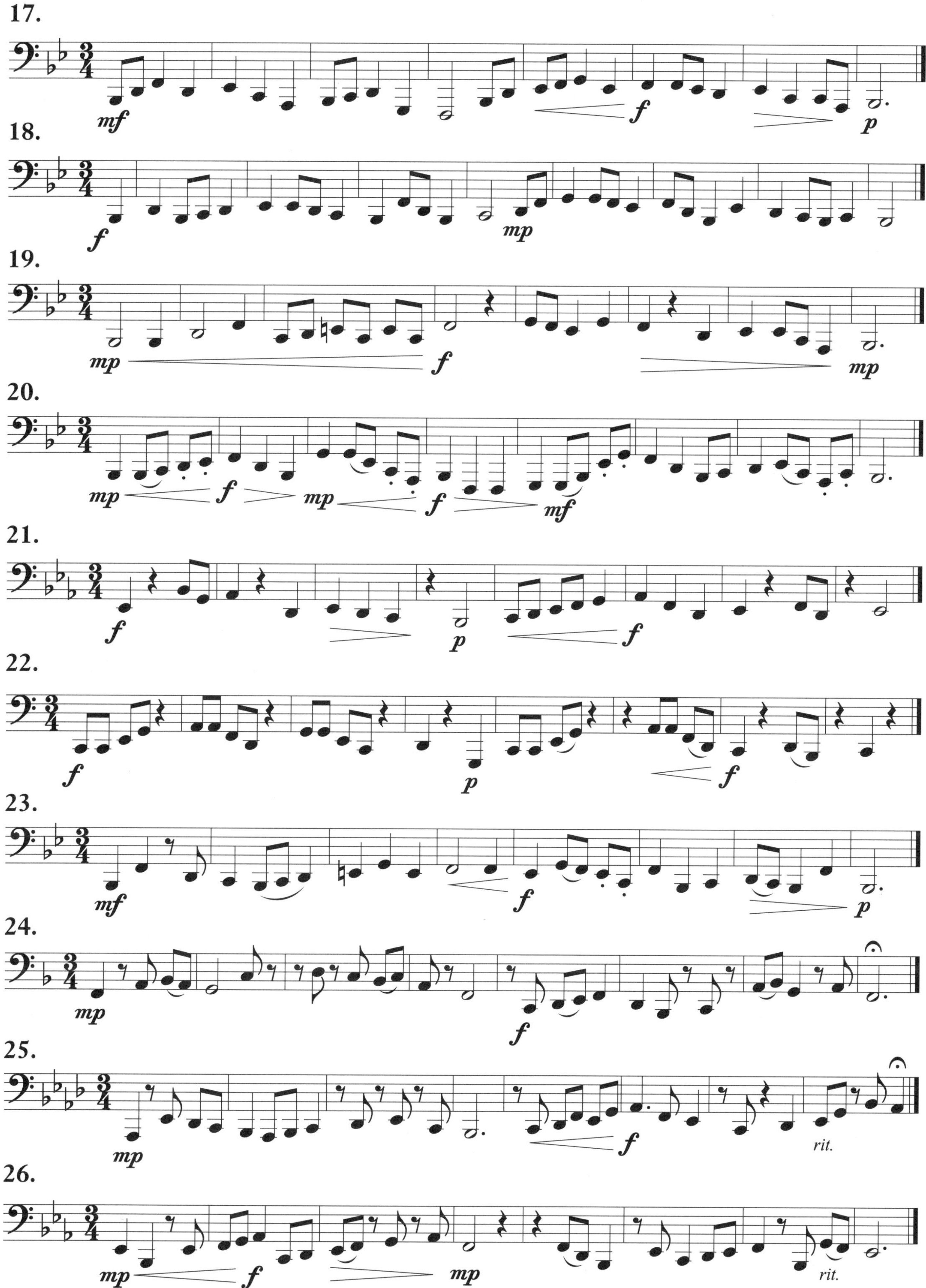
17.
mf
f
p
18.
f
mp
19.
mp
f
mp
20.
mp
f
mp
f
mf
21.
f
p
f
22.
f
p
f
23.
mf
f
p
24.
mp
f
25.
mp
f
rit.
26.
mp
f
mp
rit.

27.
mf
f
p
28.
mp
f
29.
p
mf
p
f
rit.
p
30.
mp
f
f
31.
f
mf
p
f
p
32.
p
mf
p
mf
p
f
33.
mf
p
rit.

34.
p
f
mp
f
rit.
35.
mf
f
36.
mp
mf
f
37.
mp
f
mp
38.
f
(♮)
mp
39.
f
p
mp
f

40.
mf
mp
f
rit.
41.
mf
f
mf
p
f
42.
mf
43.
3
f
p
f
p
44.
3
f
45.
mf

46.
mf
f
mp
f
mp
47.
f
mp
f
48.
mp
f
mp
f
mp
49.
mf
f
p
50.
mp
f
51.
mp
ff
mp
ff
52.
mf
53.
mf
f
p
f
p

54.
p
mf
f
55.
f
p
mf
56.
p
mf
f
p
57.
mp
f
58.
mf
p
f
p
59.
f
mp
rit.

60.
f
p
f
61.
mf
f
p
f
rit.
p
62.
f
p
f
rit.
63.
mp
f
rit.
64.
mf
p
f
rit.
a tempo
p
65.
mf
p
f
66.
f
mp
f
p
f
67.
mf
f
mp

68.
mp
f
69.
mf
70.
mf
f
71.
mf
p
f
p
mf
p
72.
mp
f
rit.
73.
mf
p
f
rit.
74.
f
mp
mf
f
rit.
75.
f
p
rit.

76.
f
mp
f
77.
p
mf
p
mf
p
mf
p
78.
f
p
f
rit.
79.
f
p
80.
mp
f
mp
mf
mp
81.
mf
mp
rit.
f
82.
f
rit.
a tempo
rit.

83.
mf
f
mp
f
mf
rit.
84.
mp
mf
f
rit.
p
85.
simile
mf
p
f
mp
rit.
86.
f
mp
f
rit.
87.
f
mp
rit.
88.
f
89.
mp
f
mp
f
mp

90.
f
rit.
91.
mf
p
f
p
92.
f
93.
mp
rit.
f
mp
94.
mf
95.
mf
96.
mp
f
mp
97.
mf
f
p

98.
mf
mp
sub. f
mp
f
99.
mp
mf
f
mp
rit.
100.
mp
f
mp
101.
mf
102.
mp
f
103.
mp
f
104.
mp
mf
mp
mf
mp

105.
f
mp
f
106.
mp
f
107.
f
3
a tempo
p
rit.
mp
p
f
ff